GETTING INTO
PRO BASEBALL

GETTING INTO PRO
BASEBALL

BY MIKE DYER

GETTING INTO THE PROS

FRANKLIN WATTS • NEW YORK • LONDON • 1979

Photographs courtesy of the St. Louis Cardinals: pp. 5, 35, and 65; the Philadelphia Phillies: pp. 2, 36, and 41; the Cincinnati Reds: pp. 8, 27, and 58; Howard Bass: p. 15; St. John's University: p. 18; the Cleveland Indians: p. 28; the New York Yankees: pp. 29 and 63; the San Diego Padres: pp. 49 and 75; the Milwaukee Brewers: p. 54; the Los Angeles Dodgers: p. 57; the Chicago Cubs: pp. 55 and 62; the Chicago White Sox: p. 76; and photographer Richard Lee: pp. 9, 10, 16, 23, 24, 32, 42, 46, 50, 61, and 66.

Library of Congress Cataloging in Publication Data

Dyer, Mike.
    Getting into pro baseball.

    (Getting into the pros)
    Includes index.
    SUMMARY: Advice for the would-be major league baseball player.
    1. Baseball—Vocational guidance—Juvenile literature. [1. Baseball—Vocational guidance. 2. Vocational guidance] I. Title.
GV867.5.D93   796.357′023   78–23181
ISBN 0–531–01319–7

CONTENTS

This book is dedicated to my parents, Blanche and Leo, who used to stand with me through doubleheaders at the old Polo Grounds, and my wife Carol, who endures 162 games each season.

There are also special thanks, in alphabetical order, to George Brett, Lou Brock, Joe Frazier, Ken and Susan Gordon, Tim Johnson, Bill Madlock, Lynn McGlothen, Dick Moss, Bots Nekola, Fred Patek, Matt Snell, Rich Tappin, Joe Torre, Dave Winfield . . . and of course, to Franklin Watts and my photographer, Rich Lee.

Mike Dyer

GETTING INTO
PRO BASEBALL

THE MODERN GAME OF BASEBALL

The locker room is alive with a sound all its own three hours before game time. In one corner there are a few athletes autographing baseballs. In another corner sit some players reading mail or playing cards. The rest are just standing around, listening to music blaring from a radio. This is how it is now, how it has been for a long time, and how it will probably be for years to come.

But there have been many changes in baseball since the game was first played in Abner Doubleday's time. Artificial turf has replaced grass in many parks. Uniforms have lost the baggy look and are now made from double-knits; the Chicago White Sox even wore shorts in 1976. In Houston and Seattle, the game is played indoors. American League designated hitters take the place of pitchers in the batting order. Players now travel by jet, and big league games are contested coast-to-coast, in Canada as well as in the U.S.

ALL SIZES AND SHAPES

Major leaguers come in a variety of sizes and shapes. But they all either hit the ball hard or throw it hard. Unlike performers in football and basketball, baseball players aren't always big. Kansas City Royals' shortstop Fred Patek is still called "Shorty," but he's learned

to live with it. Fred still remembers the games he was left out of as a child because of his size. He was even picked on and called unflattering names.

"I get many letters from boys and girls who are small," says the 5-foot, 4-inch (1.60-m) Patek. "They ask me what they can do. I had to prove I could do the job. I strove to do better. I tell the kids they have to believe in themselves. Take an opportunity and make the best of it."

But on the other hand, 6-foot, 8-inch (2.0-m) James Rodney Richard, 6-foot, 7-inch (1.98-m) John Candelaria, and 6-foot, 6-inch (1.95-m) Ron Reed (he had a two-year hitch in the National Basketball Association) prove that height is not a handicap in baseball either—especially for pitchers.

"Pro baseball," explains New York Mets' Scout Joe Frazier, "is not a game of superstrength. Anyone with good coordination can play. It gets a boy out on his own. It allows a boy to prove himself."

MAJOR LEAGUE PLAYERS ASSOCIATION

Your ears start to pop as you ride in the elevator to the thirty-eighth floor at 375 Park Avenue in New York City. The room you are heading for is number 3808. This is the headquarters for the Major League Players Association, first organized in 1954. Marvin J. Miller is the association's executive director. It is not necessary for all players to join the association, but there is almost always 100 percent membership.

Ron Reed

Each major league manager, coach, player, and trainer must pay the association three dollars for each day he spends in the big leagues. But this seems a small price, considering that the association has been responsible for raising the minimum salary in the majors from $6,000 a year in 1967—when Miller first became director—to $21,000 a year by 1978. The organization also put together for its members a pension plan, and athletes now get about twenty-five dollars a day in meal money when they're on the road, a large increase over what they used to get.

Player Representative
When members of the Detroit Tigers have a complaint or problem, they talk to outfielder Rusty Staub. He is the team's player representative for the Players Association.

The player representative and one alternate are chosen from each team by a secret vote of the players. The job is voluntary. The representatives go to two meetings a year, one at the All-Star break and the other in the middle of the winter. At these meetings, talks usually cover new contract terms, playing conditions, and cost-of-living increases.

LITTLE LEAGUE

Before they reach their twentieth birthday, most of today's major league baseball players are already professionals. They start young, blasting baseballs on sandy ballfields and in Little League parks where

Bob Forsch

the center field fence is only 180 feet (54 m) away from the plate. Then perhaps they advance to either the Babe Ruth, Connie Mack, American Legion, or Stan Musial programs, where they first come in contact with professional scouts.

Today, there are more than 6,000 chartered members enrolled in Little League, including at least one in each American state and one in each Canadian province. There also are leagues operating in Mexico, Venezuela, Puerto Rico, Bermuda, Germany, Italy, Greece, Spain, Turkey, Japan, Saudi Arabia, France, England, Panama, and Belgium.

Little League used to be exclusively for boys. Then, in 1975, girls were allowed into the program. Now youngsters of both sexes, aged seven to twelve, participate. Each league conducts its own season, and selects all-star teams that compete in tournaments in late July. The tournament finals are held each year in Williamsport, Pennsylvania, the central headquarters and birthplace of the Little League.

Although Little League offers an organized program for youngsters—complete with ballparks and uniforms—there are problems. Many major leaguers believe there is too much emphasis on winning and not enough on learning. Many of today's big leaguers say they didn't get enough hitting practice in the Little League and had to play elsewhere.

Only recently did a Little League form in the Bahamas. "All we had were amateur leagues," says Reds' outfielder Ed Armbrister, who grew up in Nassau in the Bahamas. "I played a little high school baseball, but there weren't any good baseball facilities and the coaching was poor. I was just lucky. For three straight days a scout wanted to see me play, but I told him I was too busy painting my mother's house. I hardly knew what a World Series was until I played in one in 1975."

MAJOR LEAGUERS FROM ALL OVER

You don't have to be born in a huge American city to attract baseball scouts. In fact, you don't have to be born in the United States at all. Bert Blyleven was born in the Netherlands. Tito Fuentes and Tony Perez grew up in Cuba. Rennie Stennett and Manny Sanguillen come from Panama. Rico Carty, Cesar Geronimo, and Cesar Cedeno come from the Dominican Republic, and Venezuela is home to Enzo Hernandez and Dave Concepcion. Still others come from Mexico, the Virgin Islands, and Puerto Rico.

But most major leaguers are born either among the skyscrapers of big cities like New York—Pete Falcone, Jim Palmer, and Ken Singleton, to name a few—or the farmlands—Reggie Smith, Catfish Hunter, and Woodie Fryman, for example. From his thirty-acre farm in Grand Forks, North Dakota, Tim Johnson got his first taste of baseball. "I remember pitching in the hay," says the Toronto Blue Jays' second baseman. "Really, there was little else to do. I played baseball right on the farm."

Warm weather and numerous baseball programs make living in California a big plus. The top ten states for producing major league talent in 1978 were, in order,

Over left: Tony Perez
Over right: Cesar Cedeno

California, Ohio, New York, Texas, Pennsylvania, Illinois, Alabama, Florida, North Carolina, and Massachusetts.

EDUCATION AND THE BIG LEAGUES

Many of today's ballplayers are well educated. Meeting ballplayers who hold advanced degrees from large universities is not unusual. Doc Medich, a Texas Rangers pitcher, is studying at the University of Pittsburgh School of Medicine. He has already received his bachelor of science degree in chemistry. Ex-pitcher Dave Giusti holds a master's degree in physical education from Syracuse University. San Francisco Giants' shortstop Roger Metzger was a math major at St. Edward's University in Austin, Texas.

"I can go into computer sciences after my playing days are over," he says.

At the age of thirty-five, when most people are just achieving some degree of success in their field of work, baseball players must look for something new. Many continue in the sports industry, working as coaches, managers, or sportscasters. Others leave sports to become stockbrokers, salesmen, or even movie and television stars. In fact, the trend today, more than ever before, is for ballplayers to prepare for the end of their athletic careers before it comes, by getting an education in another field.

Doc Medich

UP FROM THE SANDLOTS

THE DRAFT

Refreshments rest on a table next to a window. The plates on the table are filled with salami, swiss cheese, potato salad, rolls, and chocolate cake. Nearby are cans of soft drink.

Six men and one woman, all members of the National Association of Professional Baseball Leagues, sit around a long mahogany table, nibbling on sandwiches. The woman, who is secretary for the association, holds an index file. Names of all eligible players are in the box—all graduating high school athletes as well as those who have completed at least two years of college—are listed. In the center of the table is a telephone with a speaker.

"The Toronto Blue Jays," a voice suddenly announces over the phone, "pick . . . ," and a name is given. The athlete's position, age, height, weight, education, and hometown are also reported. This ballplayer has been selected in the free agent draft.

Twice a year—once in January and once again in June—the best baseball prospects in the world are chosen in the free agent draft. The meeting place is the sixteenth floor at 75 Rockefeller Center in New York City, the Office of the Baseball Commissioner. Each major league club is kept in touch with that office by a special telephone hookup. The team with the poorest playing record the previous year gets to choose first in the draft; the defending world champion selects last. These drawings usually go on for two days, lasting for about forty rounds. Then the teams have up to fifteen days before the next draft to sign the players to contracts. Athletes who do not sign can be chosen again in the next draft.

Teams go to a great deal of trouble to decide who to draft. Each major league club employs a squad of scouts who look over the young talent. Scouts don't often attend Little League games, but they do make the rounds at high school and college contests. Usually they can be spotted behind the plate holding a scorebook or a stopwatch and checking each player. The notes they take are later turned over to the team's front office.

CENTRALIZED SCOUTING

In the southern California city of Newport Beach there is an amazing computer. Its job is to help the Major League Scouting Bureau, sometimes referred to as "central scouting," service the eighteen big league teams that use it.

A staff of seventy scouts does the fieldwork for the Scouting Bureau. The information they gather for the semiannual drafts is fed into the computer at Newport Beach and relayed by the computer system to the participating clubs. Each team gets daily reports from the bureau.

Athletes aged sixteen to twenty-one are scouted and rated. The rating ranges from zero to eight. Those rated zero to four are considered poor prospects. Big League teams using this information may send the data to their own scouts, who often then check out the prospects themselves.

A typical scout is Francis "Bots" Nekola, who pitched for the New York Yankees when Babe Ruth and Lou Gehrig were in their prime. Now Nekola scouts for the Boston Red Sox. Among others, he signed both Carl Yastrzemski and Rico Petrocelli to Bosox contracts.

"Before central scouting," says Nekola, "I'd hire ten bird dogs [part-time scouts] to look at prospects. But the Red Sox don't have that money available anymore. It's costing the team about $200,000 a year to be part of central scouting."

With thirty years' experience as a scout, Nekola knows his job. People listen when he talks. He has these tips for high school ballplayers who have been chosen in the free agent draft and are considering a career in professional baseball:

● If you are a fringe player—someone who has athletic ability, but is also academically inclined—go to a four-year college.

● If you are a little better than fringe but a doubtful major leaguer, go to a junior college. This way you can either transfer after one or two years to a four-year college or sign with a professional team.

● If you are offered a bonus of at least $35,000, you are a prospect for the big leagues. Sign and start a career in pro baseball. You can get college credits in the off season.

TRYOUT CAMP

The scouting system isn't perfect. Once in a great while someone who should have doesn't show up in the early scouting reports. So the Major League Scout-

Baseball scouts doing their job

ing Bureau as well as the big league teams run their own tryout camps, to which they invite players.

Not much publicity is given to these tryout camps. The teams usually invite less than sixty high school and college athletes to each session. From May to July, the scouts move from town to town looking for prospects. Those invited to the camps are offered tips on hitting, pitching, and fielding, and then divided into teams for a game. Every move the athletes make is carefully watched by the scouts.

Bake McBride showed up for a tryout in Busch Stadium. His high school in Fulton, Missouri, didn't have a baseball team, so his name didn't show up in the early scouting reports. The St. Louis Cardinals, who liked what they saw, were able to wait for the thirty-seventh round in the June 1970 free agent draft to choose McBride because they knew no other team had seen him play. Four years later McBride was the National League Rookie of the Year.

Sometimes even showing up for one tryout isn't enough. New York Mets' infielder Doug Flynn was never drafted. He played softball five nights a week in his hometown of Lexington, Kentucky, and scouts never saw him play baseball. But in 1971 he was given a contract after attending four different Cincinnati tryout camps. By 1975 Flynn was with the Reds and playing in Riverfront Stadium.

COLLEGE BASEBALL

Very few major leaguers go straight from high school to professional baseball. About two out of every three

Bake McBride

in the majors now spend at least one year in college. But of the 459 major leaguers in 1978 who started college, only 94 remained long enough to collect a degree from a four-year institution.

And again, there's that California advantage— more 1976 big leaguers attended college in California than in any other state. Following California, in order, were Arizona, Florida, Michigan, Texas, Illinois, Louisiana, Washington, New York, and Pennsylvania. The eight states that failed to graduate from college a single 1978 big leaguer were Hawaii, Alaska, Maine, South Dakota, Vermont, North Dakota, Montana, and Delaware.

Arizona State, whose graduates include Sal Bando, Reggie Jackson, Craig Swan, and Len Randle, has sent the most alumni to the big leagues. Because of its near-perfect weather all year round, Arizona State plays as many as 110 games a year. Six new scholarships are offered there each year, and nearly every athlete on the roster is given at least some financial assistance.

Not far behind Arizona State with successful programs are USC, California State University, UCLA, University of Texas, University of Arizona, Michigan State, Southern University, Grambling College, and University of Tampa. Other baseball-oriented colleges are Kent State, St. John's University (New York), Florida State, Eastern Michigan University, University of South Carolina, and University of Miami (Florida). Two-year schools that qualified the most 1978 major

College baseball at St. John's University in New York

leaguers are Miami-Dade Junior College, Mesa Community College, and Los Angeles Harbor College. See the chapter "Looking for a Baseball Scholarship?" for a more complete listing of schools.

The End of the Minors?
In time, the U.S. college system could replace the minor leagues. At least that's the opinion of Richard Tappin, the successful baseball coach at New York Institute of Technology in Old Westbury, New York.

Tappin points out that professional football and basketball players are groomed through college ball. "Major league teams want to save money," he says. "It only makes sense to take the best talent from the college campuses." But Tappin rules out Canadian colleges because they don't get enough of the warm weather suitable for baseball.

Tappin, whose Tech teams won the Eastern College Athletic Conference title in 1975, 1976 and 1977, believes four-year colleges offer baseball prospects the best opportunity to face superior pitching and hitting. He says in varsity college ball, a seventeen-year-old batter can hit against a twenty-one-year-old pitcher, something that can't happen on the junior college level.

"Different kids mature at different rates," he adds. "In college, we develop pitchers. They're not just throwers. They are taught how to care for their arm. There's individual attention for all. The twenty-fifth man on my roster gets just as much practice as the best player."

GETTING INTO SHAPE FOR THE BIG LEAGUES

DAILY EXERCISING

Six hours before the opening pitch of each game, New York Yankees' trainer Gene Monahan is busy in the club's locker room. His job is to keep the athletes in tip-top shape. "Boys of Little League age don't have to do much exercising," says Monahan. "They're usually pretty busy playing sports. Swimming and running are the best things they can do to stay healthy."

Monahan frowns on exercises such as push-ups and sit-ups for youngsters. "The best thing they can do is stretch. Bring those hands overhead and reach for the sky. Work on the arms and legs. Strengthen the hamstrings."

Exercise routines in the big leagues vary from team to team. Across town from the Yankees, the Mets run a series of limbering-up drills before batting practice each day. The session starts with ballplayers windmilling their arms while their feet are in place. Next, they strengthen their hamstrings by standing with their feet wide apart and applying pressure first to one leg and then to the other. After that, they go down flat on their backs and raise their legs in the air. Sit-ups are followed by a touching of the toes and jumping jacks. Then it's time for some laps in the outfield before the signal is given to grab a bat and hit.

Kansas City Royals' manager Whitey Herzog feels that kids ten to twelve years old refuse to extend themselves. "They don't warm up properly, don't run enough, and don't throw enough. During practice, they don't extend their arms and legs. There are no sore arms if they warm up five minutes and then stretch out the throws. I've seen in my rookie camps where the boys don't throw farther than 30 feet [9 m]. They have to throw farther."

GETTING INTO SHAPE FOR PITCHING

Lynn McGlothen sees nothing wrong with Little Leaguers experimenting with a curve ball. "I've heard people say that kids aren't supposed to throw curve balls until they're in their teens," says the Cubs' pitcher. "But I threw curves when I was eight years old, and it never hurt my arm."

"You *can* hurt your arm throwing too many fastballs," he adds. "Look at some of the fastball pitchers in the major leagues. They start slowing down with age."

Fastball pitcher Tom Seaver of the Reds shares McGlothen's opinion. "I've had no problems," says the three-time Cy Young Award winner. "I threw curves when I was ten years old. But then again, you don't hear about major leaguers who do have problems."

Tom Seaver can touch his right shoulder with his right hand. Andy Messersmith, who was curving when he was eleven, says he can't do that anymore.

Tom Seaver

"My arm hurts when I try that," states Messer-smith, a member of the Yankees. "The curve puts a tremendous pressure on the elbow."

St. Louis Cardinals' pitching coach Claude Osteen threw a curve ball at the age of six. "I was just this high," he claims, holding his left hand close to the ground. "I don't advise Little Leaguers to throw curves, but my father showed me how to do it. My dad also stressed how to take care of the arm. I know how to warm up properly. I cover my arm when I'm not pitching. And after a game, I put ice on the arm. The ice stops the capillary bleeding going on inside. It speeds up recovery."

Yankee pitcher Catfish Hunter says, "Before a start, I loosen up my legs as well as my right arm. I can't field a ball properly unless I come off the mound fast. And if I come off too quickly without the right warm-up, I'm liable to pull a muscle."

Hunter runs every day between starts, usually about fifteen laps in the outfield. The day before a start he checks out the mound. Then, the second day after a start, he throws for about ten minutes on the sidelines.

GETTING IN SHAPE
FOR CATCHING

Today, the catcher's chest protector and shin guards weigh less than 2 pounds (.9 kg). The combination of fiber glass and nylon offers plenty of protection. But the catcher is still left unprotected in several places. His

Catfish Hunter

bare hand and the area just above the ankles often get nicked by foul balls.

Cincinnati Reds' all-star catcher Johnny Bench says the most important thing future catchers can do is to develop the arm. "The throw to second base is the longest one they will make," Bench points out. "It's 120 feet [30.5 m] from the plate to second. As a boy, I practiced throwing 150 feet [45 m] to stretch out the arm."

When there's no runner on base, Bench and other catchers place their throwing hand behind their back to avoid foul tips. The secret to playing behind the plate, says Hall of Famer Yogi Berra, is to have good hands. "You've got to protect your hands from foul tips," says the Yankees' coach. "Close your fingers, but don't make a hard fist. Just hold the fingers loosely."

REST AND GOOD FOOD

You can't play baseball if you are tired, so try to get at least eight hours of sleep each night. Smoking slows you down and cuts down on your wind, so avoid it altogether.

Cut down on sweets, too. Avoid the ice cream parlor with its high-calorie sodas. Eat lots of meats, vegetables, and salads instead. This is what most major leaguers eat before a game.

Opposite: Johnny Bench
Over left: Frank Duffy
Over right: Yogi Berra

BASEBALL SUMMER CAMPS

Hoping to improve their game, thousands of teen-agers attend baseball camps in the summer. Some even go to camps in the winter. Their goal is to sharpen their baseball skills. The biggest of these camps are found in Florida. They are usually open for athletes between the ages of eight and twenty, and are usually quite expensive, costing between $200 and $250 a week.

The better camps provide pitching machines and cages, big league training facilities, major league instructors, and a schedule of games. But there are too many examples of poor baseball camps. "In many of these camps," says New York Tech coach Richard Tappin, "they just give boys bats and balls and let them play before and after lunch. Very rarely do you see a boy return to that kind of camp for a second year."

So if you are thinking of going to one of these camps, investigate carefully what it offers before you decide.

THE BUSINESS OF BECOMING A PRO

THE CONTRACT

Parachuting, skydiving, and automobile and motor-cycle racing are out. Also say farewell to fencing, boxing, wrestling, karate, judo, football, basketball, skiing, hockey, and any other sport or activity involving a substantial risk of personal injury. Once you've signed a contract, you can't participate in any other amateur, intramural, intercollegiate, or professional sport without the written consent of the club.

That's all spelled out in your six-page Uniform Player Contract, the contract you must sign to begin your career as a professional baseball player. You also must sell any stock or financial interest you may have in any other professional team. You will be required to undergo an extensive physical and dental examination. On the agreed date, you must report to your assigned team. And in case of injury while playing, you will receive free surgical, medical, and hospital services.

For your loyalty and services the team pays you a salary (usually on the first and fifteenth day of each month) and provides a baseball uniform and transportation from home to road games. During the training season, the club also pays for traveling, food, and lodging.

BONUSES

The best baseball prospects each year get something extra for signing their contract: a bonus. This bonus could range from several hundred dollars to several hundred thousand dollars, depending on your baseball credentials. If the bonus is more than fifty thousand dollars, it is best to work out the arrangements of payment with a good attorney.

Some prospects believe they will get a bigger bonus if they play hard to get. Sometimes the gamble pays off. Other times, an athlete can lose out altogether. If you get into such a situation, think before you act.

AGENTS

Fresh out of high school, eighteen-year-old Jeff Burroughs was the nation's number one selection in the June 1969 free agent draft. He agreed to an $88,000 bonus from the Washington Senators to sign his contract and spent three years in the minor leagues before becoming a Texas Ranger. He didn't use an agent for his salary negotiations. "It wasn't necessary," says Burroughs. "There isn't much an agent can do during negotiations except collect his 15 percent."

Burroughs says the government is going to get a large chunk of the bonus anyway. "Let's face it," adds the American League's 1974 Most Valuable Player, "if you make it to the major leagues, that bonus is very little in comparison to your salary. You can make thirty times that bonus in the majors."

Pete Rose

During his college days at Ohio State, Matt Snell wasn't even supposed to know an agent. "Woody Hayes wouldn't allow one on campus," the onetime New York Jets' football star comments. Snell is now president of the Bradcor Sports Services of Jericho, New York. Among other things, he acts as an agent for baseball players.

"It would be incomplete to say we are just negotiators," says John Doering, Bradcor's vice-president. "We have a complete setup that includes investments for our clients, real estate, mortgages, off-season employment, television commercials, and public relations opportunities."

Long before the athletes are selected in the free agent draft, people from Snell's outfit—like other agents —make contact with baseball prospects. "We ask for only 5 percent and we are well worth it," states Snell. "We know what a player, say on the sixth round, is really worth."

In most cases, you don't have to look for an agent. The agent will find you first. The fee ranges from 5 to 15 percent of your contract.

Don Balsamo, former minor league player and now a baseball agent for Bradcor Sports Services, thinks that recently drafted players need agents the most. "It's the same in all sports," he comments. "Some ballplayers aren't careful the way they talk. They must be warned. Others act too timid and shy. Remember, only one out of every 1,200 boys in organized baseball will make it to the major leagues. There is a lot of competition. The athletes should concentrate on playing, and we'll handle the money part."

Al Hrabosky

There are good agents, and there are bad ones. Be sure about who you choose.

YOUR SUITCASE
IS PACKED

The contract is signed. The agent is paid. You've said goodbye to family and friends. Now you're a professional, and your next stop is a minor league town.

Mike Schmidt

WAHCONAH PARK: WELCOME TO THE MINORS

A high wire fence is the only thing that separates the parking lot from the playing field. In back of the stadium, in dead center field, is the winding Housatonic River. The stadium itself is 331 feet (99 m) down the right field line, 349 feet (111.7 m) down the left field line, and only 345 feet (103.5 m) to straightaway center. Just below the right field scoreboard is a sign wishing the team success—from the U.S. Army Recruiting Center. This is Wahconah Park in Pittsfield, Massachusetts, where AA minor league baseball is played.

A professional team called the Berkshire Brewers plays its Eastern League games in this stadium. Only the athletes' uniforms look big league. Missing from the ballpark are hot dog sellers, ushers, security people, and—most of all—fans. There are only two umpires to a game and the national anthem is played by a tiny cassette tape recorder held close to a microphone in the antiquated press box.

Sam Hinds is a pitcher from Fresno, California. Dan Thomas, an outfielder, hails from Mobile, Alabama. Outfielder Dick Davis is from Compton, California. Barry Cort, another pitcher, was raised in Tampa, Florida. John Felske, the manager, is a former catcher for the Chicago Cubs and Milwaukee Brewers. In the summer of 1976, these people and others were brought together as members of the Berkshire Brewers, a minor league team under a working agreement with the Milwaukee Brewers of the American League.

When he signed for a bonus of about $50,000, Dan Thomas thought he had it made. He was the top 1972 selection of the Milwaukee Brewers after an excellent career in Little League, high school, and American Legion ball. He thought he had so much money, he could give some away. But he married young and soon learned how fast money can be spent. "When I signed with the Brewers, I said, 'I'm now a professional.' I thought I'd never see a dirty baseball again," he explained.

But Thomas had to be out every day, drilling, fielding ground balls, and taking plenty of batting practice. Baseball isn't what Dan Thomas thought it would be like. It's not always fun; it's also work, lots of work. In 1976 Thomas led the Eastern League in batting, home runs, and runs batted in. His work was rewarded when he was made a member of the Milwaukee Brewers in 1977. But that didn't last long either.

Dick Davis lives just a few blocks from Wahconah Park. As he travels to the stadium each day, he passes unrecognized, just a blur on the street. Davis spent one year in college at the University of Utah in Salt Lake City, then signed for a bonus of about $20,000. In 1975, his third year in professional baseball, he led the Eastern League in homers. Yet, he was in the same league in 1976 and discouraged. Davis claims he will quit the game if he doesn't move up the ladder faster.

Molding the Brewers is the job of John Felske, who is not much older than the athletes. Besides managing, Felske also pitches batting practice and acts as coach. He has no other help. There is a month of spring training. The Brewers must play 140 games from mid-April to early September. There are only two scheduled off-days all season for the athletes.

Seventy of the team's games are on the road. The team goes as far north as the city of Quebec in Canada, and as far south as Williamsport, Pennsylvania. Felske understands how the traveling drains energy from his team. There are times when they arrive in a town at two or three in the morning, following an all-night bus trip, and are told the hotel is filled. The players must wait in the bus until there are rooms available in the hotel.

Crowded Quarters
Sam Hinds, 6-foot, 7-inches (1.97-m), has to lower his head when he enters the Berkshire clubhouse. The team's twenty-one athletes, crowded into a tiny locker room, have little space even for breathing, let alone dressing. Even the sodas aren't free. It's a little better in AAA where the soda is available in the locker room, but the players get billed for it at the end of each month.

The area the trainer works in is even worse than the dressing area. Rows of aspirin, baby oil, and foot powder containers rest on shelves surrounding the rubbing table. The bathroom sink is nearly hidden by hairdryers, towels, and a variety of hair products. The sign over the front door from the National Association of Professional Baseball Leagues, whose headquarters are in St. Petersburg, Florida, urges athletes to make sure they have a copy of their contract, and to stay away from illegal drugs. "Possession or distribution of amphetamines and barbiturates is a violation of federal and state laws," warns the sign.

Tug McGraw

THE MINOR LEAGUE SYSTEM

For many years in baseball most big league teams had working agreements with fifteen to twenty minor league teams each. Then, due to the television boom beginning in the 1950s, people stopped buying tickets to minor league games and stayed home to watch the televised major league games instead.

With the cost of living rising and fewer people at minor league ballparks, major league clubs were forced to sever their ties with the lower minor league classifications. Those minor leagues which had the least talent and money were forced out of business.

By 1978, only twenty minor leagues remained. Including play in the Mexican League (AAA), the Mexican Central League (A), and the Mexican Pacific Coast League (A), there were only about 160 teams on the North American continent.

Class A is made up of ten leagues. A player in A ball makes only $600 a month. When on the road, he is paid only $6 a day in meal money, and the meals are usually eaten in some fast-food restaurant.

The Class A leagues include the California League, the Carolina League (with teams from North Carolina, South Carolina, and Virginia), the Florida State League, the Midwest League (Iowa, Wisconsin, and Illinois), the New York-Penn League, the Northwest League (Oregon, Washington, and Idaho), the Western Carolina League (South Carolina, North Carolina, and Virginia), the Appalachian League (Tennessee, Virginia, and West Virginia), the Gulf Coast League (Florida), and the Pioneer League (Montana, Idaho, and Alberta, Canada).

Thurman Munson

If an athlete shows promise, he is promoted to AA baseball, where his salary is usually $800 a month and the meal money is $7.50 a day. The Eastern League (Connecticut, Massachusetts, Pennsylvania, and Canada), the Texas League, and the Southern League (Alabama, Tennessee, North Carolina, and Georgia) are the only AA classification leagues.

The minor league picture is brighter in the AAA level, an athlete's last stop before the big leagues. Most teams in AAA travel by chartered plane. Salaries are also better here, ranging from about $15,000 to $25,000 a year. Leagues making up the AAA division are the American Association (Indiana, Nebraska, Iowa, Colorado, Kansas, and Oklahoma), the International League (Virginia, New York, West Virginia, Tennessee, Rhode Island, and Ohio), and the Pacific Coast League (Utah, Arizona, New Mexico, California, and Washington).

THE LEARNING PROCESS

The minor leaguer's job is to learn. Batting and pitching instructors accompany many teams. Even a simple game of pepper—an exercise ballplayers perform before every game—is treated like a ninth-inning drill.

Nearly every major leaguer has performed in a minor league city like Pittsfield. It's a learning experience for most.

Lynn McGlothen spent parts of six years in the minors. He thinks it helped. He noted most pitchers already have a fastball and curve when they're signed.

The game of pepper

"But, in the minors, it's learning what to throw and when that is important," says the Cubs' pitcher. "I wasn't a 'thinking pitcher' until then. It's not just throwing strikes. By the time you reach Triple A, you should be a thinking pitcher."

Twins' pitcher Jerry Koosman agrees. "In the minors, I learned a curve ball is not an inshoot. I developed a slider and change-up to go with my fastball. We always practiced pick-off moves, making refinements."

Boston Red Sox outfielder Jim Rice, who spent four years in the minors, says it made him a better player. "When you play high school or American Legion ball, you work on fundamentals. But with a professional team, you move around and learn overall team play. Besides travel, you also gain maturity. It's being a man. You're away from home, and have a chance to grow up faster."

A Bad Experience for Some

But for some, playing in the minor leagues has been a bad experience—or even worse, a waste of time.

Living conditions can be awful. Don Balsamo, formerly of the Detroit Tigers, remembers boarding in Army barracks in Lakeland, Florida. RAF blankets covered his bed. "In two and a half weeks, I dropped from 222 to 204 pounds," he recalls. "There was breakfast before nine o'clock, practice at ten, lunch, and then another practice at two o'clock. We had an early curfew."

There is a sadness in San Diego pitcher Mickey

Jerry Koosman

Lolich's voice when he talks of his four years in the minors. "I didn't learn a thing," he said of his minor league training. "I was never taught how to pitch. No one talked to me down there. And the traveling was terrible. I remember going from Knoxville to Jacksonville by bus. It took seventeen hours and there was no air conditioning. We'd leave the park after a night game and travel all night and into the following day. We'd pull into our destination at three o'clock the next afternoon and play that night."

Missing the Minors Completely
Dave Winfield heard so many stories about the minor leagues, he jumped straight from the college campus to the majors. He was named first team All-America in 1973 at the University of Minnesota, and selected Most Valuable Player in the College World Series. But the 6-foot, 6-inch (1.95-m) Winfield was also drafted by the Minnesota Vikings to play pro football, and the Utah Stars and Atlanta Hawks drafted him to play pro basketball. "I never wanted to go to the minors and I told the Padres that," he explains. "They really had no choice if they wanted me."

Even today, Winfield is not sure he did the right thing. "It may have hurt me in the beginning so I wouldn't recommend it to anyone else," says the outfielder. "The traveling in the majors didn't bother me since I had gone barnstorming to places like Alaska and Hawaii with semipro teams. But it was difficult getting used to the pitchers. Some threw pitches I had never seen before. It's extra hard to develop consistency when you're in a spot like that."

Dave Winfield

WAITING FOR THE BIG DAY

Walla Walla, West Palm Beach, and Billings, Montana, may be nice places to visit, but baseball players don't want to stay there. Their goal is the major leagues. The big league teams have an investment in these minor leaguers also, and are continually checking on the progress the athletes are making.

So minor leaguers anxiously await the happy day when the manager tells the athlete he should pack his suitcase because he's going to the big leagues. For many players, that first call comes around the first of September, when the minor league season is coming to a close and the big league team can expand its roster from twenty-five to forty players. Or it may come in the winter draft, at which time the player is told to report to the big league team the following spring.

Then, the hamburgers turn into steaks. The hotels are suddenly the best ones in the city. The clubhouses are spacious, carpeted locker rooms. The bus rides become trips on 747s. The crowds are boisterous, and the fans want autographs. Newspaper stories about you are read all over town. That once-in-a-lifetime opportunity has come. You're a big leaguer!

Al Oliver

SOME TIPS FROM THE STARS

BATTING

Athletes are serious about the kind of bat they wave at the pitcher. Willie Mays says too many youngsters select a bat only because their favorite player's name is on it. Says Mays, "The most important thing about a bat is that it feels comfortable to you."

The batting glove—actually it's a golf glove—is the "in" thing with major leaguers today. But Kansas City Royals' third baseman George Brett won't be seen with one. "I can't feel the bat," says the American League's 1976 batting champion. "I can't get a good grip."

Brett, whose older brothers Ken, John, and Bob all played professional baseball, remembers his conditioning as a boy. "One of the first things I can remember using was a batting tee. Sometimes we hung a ball from the garage rafters and took swings at it. We hit that ball squarely."

As a youngster, Henry Aaron batted cross-handed. He changed his style and rewrote the major league home run record. "Just keep swinging," says the future Hall of Famer who hung up his spikes in 1976. "My power is in the wrists, but that doesn't mean everyone has power there. You have to feel comfortable at the plate, and keep swinging."

Going to the plate "scared" is a problem shared by many Little League-age boys, according to San Francisco's infielder Bill Madlock. "You can't be afraid of the ball," says Madlock, who led the National League in batting in both 1975 and 1976. "The boys wear protective helmets in Little League. The ball may hit them, but it won't hurt much. You can't be afraid up there at the plate."

Madlock struck out only thirty-four times in 1975. "I choke up about three inches off the handle. That way I can go with the pitch, pull the ball, or go to the opposite field. Let's face it, we're not all home run hitters."

At the age of eight, Texas Rangers' outfielder John Grubb, a natural right-handed batter, experimented by swinging from the left side of the plate. He became so good at it that he made himself a permanent left-handed batter. "I'd advise all youngsters to try switch-hitting," says Grubb.

Yankee outfielder Roy White, a professional at the age of eighteen, was a switch-hitter before his twelfth birthday. Then again, Phils' shortstop Bud Harrelson didn't begin to switch-hit until he was twenty-two years old and a minor leaguer.

FIRST BASE

Watch a first baseman holding a runner on the base. His right foot is anchored to the bag. His glove is outstretched, ready for a pick-off attempt by the pitcher.

Over left: Henry Aaron
Over right: Bill Madlock

First base, according to the Mets' manager Joe Torre, is a thinking person's position. "You don't have time to think after the ball is fielded, and you can't depend on hearing the pitcher say which base to make a play at. You have to work on all the possibilities ahead of time. The toughest play for me was the 3–6–3 double play, where I fielded the ball, threw to the shortstop for the force, and then took the return throw."

When a baseball is hit to left centerfield, Los Angeles Dodgers' first baseman Steve Garvey goes into motion, cutting across the infield to back up the other infielders. "That cut-off play," says the 1974 National League's Most Valuable Player, "gives me the most trouble."

Now a Yankee sportscaster, Bill White has this to say about the position: "On low throws most first basemen close their eyes anyway and hope for the best. That's not the toughest play to learn. It only looks hard." White explains that one of the most difficult plays is holding a runner on first, charging a bunt, and then making a force play at second base.

SECOND BASE

The ball hit to his right, near the bag, gives Montreal Expos' second baseman Dave Cash the most difficulty. "It's the kind of play where you reach across the body, backhand the ball, and then make the throw to first," he notes. "It's also very hard to cover first on an expected bunt play when the batter hits away instead. On a bunt the second baseman rushes to cover first. So

Steve Garvey

if the batter grounds to the shortstop, you have to back up and take the throw for the force at second."

Joe Morgan, the Reds' second baseman, suggests practicing the double play pivot as much as possible. "Just concentrate on crossing over, touching the base, and then throwing to first," he says.

THIRD BASE

The cut-off, Bill Madlock claims, is the most difficult play for a third baseman to learn. If the ball is hit to left field, the third baseman is usually the player who takes the throw in from the outfield. "But the trickiest for me," says Madlock, "is when the ball is hit between the first and second basemen. Those two infielders are out of the play and I have to cut across the infield to take the throw, in case there is a play on the hitter who takes a big turn rounding the bag."

Texas' Buddy Bell has the most trouble with the swinging bunt. "If you're playing back on the hitter, there's little you can do about it. But if you're playing in, you have to charge the ball bare-handed and in one motion throw to first sidearmed." And what about tag plays? "Just make sure the ball is in front of the bag," Bell says.

Roy Staiger, formerly of the Mets, notes he has to think quickly when there are runners on first and second and the batter bunts. He has to decide whether to charge the ball and throw to first or stay back for a play at third. "It's better to play the ball and get a sure out," says Staiger. "If there's no play at third, the batter beats it out and the bases are loaded."

Joe Morgan

SHORTSTOP

On artificial turf, shortstops now position themselves in short left field. The ball comes at them much faster, and they need a strong arm to make the toss to first.

In the field, Kansas City shortstop Fred Patek wears a golf glove on his left hand under the fielder's mitt. "The important thing," Patek says, "is that the glove fits your hand comfortably." Shortstops, he says, should concentrate most on grounders. "Practice your weak habits. Take a lot of ground balls. Find yourself a good fielder's glove. Make sure the glove isn't so deep you can't get the ball out of the pocket."

With a runner on first, the shortstop and second baseman have to be alert for a steal of second. "I give the sign to the second baseman on each pitch," said Patek, "and I decide who will cover the base. It all depends on who is up, the runner, and the kind of pitch being made to the batter."

THE OUTFIELD

When Los Angeles Dodger Rick Monday arrives at the ballpark, the center fielder immediately checks the outfield to see whether it's "fast" or "slow."

He explains: "I see if the grass has been cut recently. If it hasn't been, the ball won't roll quickly and I'll have to charge it. I also look for holes in the outfield, spots that may be tricky for me later on.

"Even the cut-offs have to be considered early. If there's a man on first base, I plan where I'm going to throw the ball if it's hit to me. I have to know how fast

Bert Campaneris

Rick Monday

Roy White

the outfield is, the speed of the runner, and how deep I'm playing. Always stay in front of the ball. If it takes a bad hop, you will still be in a position to handle it. Have the game under control."

STEALING

At the age of thirty-five, Lou Brock stole a major league record 118 bases. Since then, Brock has erased the big league record for career stolen bases.

"Just imagine stealing a base as ballet without music," says Brock. "It's all balance, the runner's balance against the pitcher's balance. When the pitcher throws, which foot moves first, the front foot or the back foot? For balance, the pitcher's back foot has to move first.

"If stealing a base was only speed, I couldn't do it at the age of thirty-eight. Only pitchers with an in-balance [very smooth in shifting their weight] can fool a good baserunner."

Curiously, the St. Louis Cardinals' outfielder says he has better success stealing against a left-handed pitcher than a right-hander. "I can see what a lefty is doing. But a right-hander has his back to me."

Brock has these pointers for future base thieves:

● With a left-handed batter at the plate and a runner on first, the catcher can't see the runner breaking. The first baseman will yell, "He's going" when the runner takes off for second base. So you yell, "He's going" on every other pitch to confuse the catcher.

Lou Brock

● If you're on third base, stand 4 to 6 inches (10 to 15 cm) in front of the base, right on the foul line. It's impossible for the catcher to see third base then from his angle, so he won't throw down because he doesn't know how much of a lead you have. Don't worry about pick-offs.

Get into foul territory once the pitch is delivered so if you're hit by the batted ball you won't be ruled out.

● You have a chance to steal a sign if you're on second base. Usually the catcher will position his glove if the next pitch is a fastball. He will not position it on a breaking ball. So you can usually tell when a fastball is coming. It's not a foolproof system, but it does work in favor of the baserunner.

● It is easier to steal third base than second base. If a right-handed batter is at the plate, he'll screen out the catcher, who then in turn is forced to step back and make the throw to third base. Of course, you also get a larger lead off second base than first base.

Willie Randolph

LOOKING FOR A BASEBALL SCHOLARSHIP?

The following is a partial list of colleges in the United States that offer baseball scholarships. They are arranged by state. If you are interested, write to the Admissions Office of the school of your choice for more details.

ARIZONA

Arizona State University, Tempe, Arizona 85281
University of Arizona, McKale Center, SUPO Box 36830, Tucson, Arizona 85721
Mesa Community College, West Southern Avenue, Mesa, Arizona 85202

CALIFORNIA

California State, 5151 State University Drive, Los Angeles, California 90032
University of California, Irvine, California 92717
University of California (UCLA), 405 Hilgard Avenue, Los Angeles, California 90024
Los Angeles Harbor Junior College, 1111 Figueroa Place, Wilmington, California 90744
Santa Clara University, Santa Clara, California 95053
University of Southern California (USC), University Park, Los Angeles, California 90007

CONNECTICUT
University of New Haven, 300 Orange Avenue, West Haven, Connecticut 06516

FLORIDA
Florida State University, Tully Gymnasium, Tallahassee, Florida 32306

Miami-Dade Community College, 11380 North West 27th Avenue, Miami, Florida 33167

University of Tampa, 401 West Kennedy Boulevard, Tampa, Florida 33606

INDIANA
Notre Dame University, Notre Dame, Indiana 46556

LOUISIANA
Grambling College, Grambling, Louisiana 71245

Southern University and A.&M., Southern Branch Post Office, Baton Rouge, Louisiana 70813

MARYLAND
University of Maryland, College Park, Maryland 20740

MICHIGAN
Eastern Michigan, Ypsilanti, Michigan 48197

Michigan State University, East Lansing, Michigan 48824

NEW JERSEY
Fairleigh Dickinson University, 1000 River Road, Teaneck, New Jersey 07666

Monmouth College, Cedar and Norwood Avenue, West Long Branch, New Jersey 07764

Rutgers University, College Avenue, New Brunswick, New Jersey 08903

Seton Hall University, 400 South Orange Avenue, South Orange, New Jersey 07079

NEW YORK
Adelphi University, South Avenue, Garden City, New York 11530

New York Institute of Technology, Post Office Box 170, Wheatley Road, Old Westbury, New York 11568

C.W. Post College, Brookville, New York 11548

St. John's University, Jamaica, New York 11439

OHIO
Bowling Green State University, Bowling Green, Ohio 43403

Kent State University, Kent, Ohio 44242

OREGON
Oregon State University, Gill Coliseum 103, Corvallis, Oregon 97331

PENNSYLVANIA
Penn State University, University Park, Pennsylvania 16802

SOUTH CAROLINA
University of South Carolina, Columbia, South Carolina 29208

TEXAS
University of Texas, Austin, Texas 78712

WASHINGTON
Washington State University, Pullman, Washington 99163

University of Washington, Seattle, Washington 98195

GUIDE TO THE MINOR LEAGUES

Below is a listing of the 16 minor leagues operating in the United States. Included are the names of the teams that play in the leagues. Each club's major league affiliation is in parentheses following the listing.

AAA CLASSIFICATION

International League
Tidewater, Va. (Mets); Rochester, N.Y. (Orioles); Syracuse, N.Y. (Yankees); Charleston, W. Va. (Astros); Richmond, Va. (Braves); Toledo, Ohio (Indians); Pawtucket, R.I. (Red Sox); Columbus, Ohio (Pirates).

American Association
Evansville, Ind. (Tigers); Indianapolis, Ind. (Reds); Omaha, Neb. (Royals); Des Moines, Iowa (White Sox); Denver, Colo. (Expos); New Orleans (Cardinals); Wichita, Kan. (Cubs); Oklahoma City, Okla. (Phillies).

Pacific Coast League
Salt Lake City, Utah (Angels); Tucson, Ariz. (Rangers); Albuquerque, N.M. (Dodgers); Phoenix, Ariz. (Giants); Hawaii (Padres); Tacoma, Wash. (Twins); Spokane, Wash. (Brewers); Sacramento, Calif. (Rangers); San Jose, Calif. (A's).

AA CLASSIFICATION

Eastern League
Reading, Pa. (Phillies); Waterbury, Conn. (Giants); Bristol, R.I. (Red Sox); Quebec, Canada (Expos); West Haven, Conn. (Yankees); Three Rivers, Canada (Reds); Jersey City, N.J. (Indians); Holyoke, Mass. (Brewers).

Southern League
Montgomery, Ala. (Tigers); Chattanooga, Tenn. (A's); Knoxville, Tenn. (White Sox); Charlotte, N.C. (Orioles); Orlando, Fla. (Twins); Savannah, Ga. (Braves); Columbus, Ga. (Astros); Jacksonville, Fla. (Royals).

Texas League
Lafayette, La. (Giants); Jackson, Miss. (Mets); Little Rock, Ark. (Cardinals); Amarillo, Tex. (Padres); Midland, Tex. (Cubs); Shreveport, La. (Pirates); El Paso, Tex. (Angels); San Antonio, Tex. (Dodgers); Tulsa, Okla. (Rangers).

A CLASSIFICATION

California League
Reno, Nev. (Twins/Padres); Visalia, Calif. (Twins); Fresno, Calif. (Giants); Lodi, Calif. (Dodgers); Salinas, Calif. (Angels); Modesto, Calif. (A's); Bakersfield, Calif. (Dodgers); San Jose, Calif. (Indians).

Carolina League
Peninsula, Va. (Phillies); Winston-Salem, N.C. (Red Sox); Salem, Va. (Pirates); Spartanburg, S.C. (Phillies); Lynchburg, Va. (Rangers); Asheville, N.C. (Rangers); Greenwood, S.C. (Braves); Charleston, S.C. (Pirates).

Florida State League
St. Petersburg (Cardinals); Tampa (Reds); Winter Haven (Red Sox); Lakeland (Tigers); Miami (Orioles);

Pompano Beach (Cubs); Fort Lauderdale (Yankees); West Palm Beach (Expos); Cocoa (Astros); Sarasota (White Sox); Daytona Beach (Royals).

Midwest League
Waterloo, Iowa (Royals); Dubuque, Iowa (Astros); Wisconsin Rapids, Wis. (Twins); Appleton, Wis. (White Sox); Wausau, Wis. (Mets); Quad Cities (Angels); Danville, Ill. (Dodgers); Burlington, Iowa (Brewers); Clinton, Iowa (Tigers); Cedar Rapids, Iowa (Giants).

New York-Penn League
Newark, N.Y. (Brewers); Elmira, N.Y. (Red Sox); Oneonta, N.Y. (Yankees); Auburn, N.Y. (Phillies); Niagara Falls, N.Y. (Pirates); Geneva, N.Y. (Cubs); Batavia, N.Y. (Indians); Utica, N.Y. (Blue Jays).

Northwest League
Bellingham, Wash. (Seattle); Eugene, Ore. (Reds); Walla Walla, Wash. (Padres); Boise, Idaho (A's).

Western Carolina League
Spartanburg, S.C. (Phillies); Shelby, N.C. (Reds); Greenwood, S.C. (Braves); Charleston, S.C. (Pirates); Ashville, N.C. (Rangers); Gastonia, N.C. (Cardinals); Salem, Va. (Pirates).

Appalachian League
Johnson City, Tenn. (Cardinals); Elizabethton, Tenn. (Twins); Bristol, Va. (Tigers); Kingsport, Tenn. (Braves); Marion, Va. (Mets); Covington, Va. (Astros); Pulaski, Va. (Phillies); Bluefield, W. Va. (Orioles).

Pioneer League
Great Falls, Mont. (Giants); Idaho Falls, Idaho (Angels); Billings, Mont. (Reds); Idaho Falls (Red Sox).

A FINAL WORD

Being a major league baseball player may seem quite glamorous—and it certainly can be. Some major leaguers receive salaries as high as $250,000 a year. They get to see the country and to appear on television. A few even get to do commercials or star in movies. But there are drawbacks.

The greatest drawback in pursuing a career in pro baseball can be seen by looking at the statistics. Major league baseball employs only about 600 players, who earn an average salary of around $45,000 a year. In the minor leagues, which employ around 3,000 players, the salaries are much lower. Also consider that there are over 35,000 nonprofessionals eligible each year for the draft, but that fewer than 1 percent of these get drafted.

Once you make it into the pros, you have to deal with lots of other problems, such as the time spent traveling away from home. Many players complain that they miss their wives and families. Some find it difficult to get used to jet lag. And it's not unheard of for a team to arrive in a town at three o'clock in the morning and have to play a game that afternoon.

In addition, many promising young players have seen their careers ended early by injuries. Leg and back injuries are common and can cause great gen-

Randy Jones

eral discomfort, even if they don't prevent the athlete from playing. And anytime someone is throwing a baseball at your head at a speed of 100 miles an hour (160 kmph)—that's dangerous!

Trades, too, have distressed athletes who thought they were going to remain with a team for their playing life. Families frequently uprooted can break apart under the strain.

And perhaps the hardest of all to take is the inevitable slowing down—when an athlete finds he can't bend as easily as he used to for ground balls or throw his fastball with the same velocity as before. At that time, somewhere around the age of thirty-five, the athlete may begin to look for his pink slip to arrive, the notice that will send him back to the minors or out on unconditional release. Then the still young but aging athlete wishes he were twenty again, and trying on his first pair of big league spikes.

Bucky Dent

INDEX

Montreal Expos, 56
Morgan, Joe, 59
Most Valuable Player Awards, 33, 48, 56

National Association of Professional Baseball Leagues, 12, 40
National League, 17, 53, 56
Nekola, Francis "Bots," 14
New York Jets, 34
New York Mets, 3, 17, 47, 56, 59
New York-Penn League, 43, 73
New York Tech, 30
Northwest League, 43, 73

Office of the Baseball Commissioner, 12
Osteen, Claude, 25
Outfield, tips on, 60, 64

Pacific Coast League, 44, 71
Palmer, Jim, 7
Patek, Fred, 1, 3, 60
Pepper, 44
Perez, Tony, 7
Petrocelli, Rico, 14
Pick-offs, 52, 67
Pioneer League, 43, 73
Pitching, 26
    and base stealing, 64
    exercise for, 22, 25
    and hitting, 48
    instruction on, 44, 47, 48, 64

Randle, Len, 19
Reed, Ron, 3
Rest, for training, 26
Rice, Jim, 47
Richard, James Rodney, 3
Riverfront Stadium, 17
Rookie of the Year, 17
Running, for exercise, 21
Ruth, Babe, 14

St. Louis Cardinals, 17, 25, 64
San Francisco Giants, 11
Sanguillen, Manny, 7

Scholarships, colleges with, 68–70
Scouting, 6–7, 13–14, 17
Seaver, Tom, 22
Second base, tips on, 56, 59, 60
Shin guards, for catcher, 26
Shortstop, tips on, 60
Singleton, Ken, 7
Slider, development of, 47
    See also Pitching
Smith, Reggie, 7
Snell, Matt, 34
Southern League, 44, 72
Staiger, Roy, 59
Stan Musial program, 6
Staub, Rusty, 4
Stealing, of bases, 60, 64, 67
Stennett, Rennie, 7
Stretching, as exercise, 21–22
Summer camps, baseball, 30
Swan, Craig, 19
Swimming, for exercise, 21
Switch-hitting, 53

Tag plays, and third base, 59
Tappin, Richard, 20, 31
Texas League, 44, 72
Texas Rangers, 11, 53
Third base, 59, 67
Thomas, Dan, 38, 39
Toronto Blue Jays, 7, 12
Torre, Joe, 56
Trades, strain from, 77
Tryout camps, 14, 17

Umpires, 38
Uniform Player Contract, 31
    See also Contracts, professional
Utah Stars, 48

Wahconah Park, 38, 39
Washington Senators, 33
Western Carolina League, 43, 73
White, Bill, 56
White, Roy, 53
Winfield, Dave, 48

Yastrzemski, Carl, 14

ABOUT THE AUTHOR

Mike Dyer is a sportswriter for the Middletown (New York) *Times-Herald Record,* and has in the past worked in the same capacity for the *Long Island Press* and the *Albany Times-Union.* Mike is a member of the Baseball Writers Association of America, and has a degree in journalism from Hofstra University, where he founded and was editor of the alumni newspaper.

Mike admits his favorite hobby is still sports, even though he deals with it professionally every day. But he is also interested in music and the occult.